WE WERE MORE
THAN KINDLING

WE WERE MORE
THAN KINDLING

POEMS

Jessica Morey-Collins

BLACK LAWRENCE PRESS

Black Lawrence Press

Executive Editor: Diane Goettel
Chapbook Editor: Lisa Fay Coutley
Book Cover and Interior Design: Zoe Norvell

ISBN: 978-1-62557-065-9

Published 2023 by Black Lawrence Press.
Printed in the United States.

for survivors

and for Riley, who takes exquisite care
with my no and my yes

TABLE OF CONTENTS

PASSAGE

By the time I got home, the raccoon had chewed through
the hen's neck and fled. The remaining brood was shriek-
ing in their coop. Cycling back from campus, I had listened
to paraphrased accounts of people who survived the East
Area Rapist-Original Night Stalker (EAR-ONS): *blindfold,
lotion pump, Coors can*. I devour these stories like I'll cal-
lous. My roommates hovered in the yard, shovel, broom, and
un-thrown stone at the ends of slack arms, eyes trained on
the raccoon clinging to a high tree branch. Blood wet feath-
ers parted to expose puckered skin and tooth punctures.
Years ago, a philosopher whispered *isn't this natural* while he
dipped his fingers in my inert body. Amazing the way a tiny
wound, precisely placed, can devastate. Who hasn't aspired
to a thicker skin? Only one year later, my future husband will
press me against a cedar between graves, and wet and not
yet dead, I will allow him to love me. But the next day, I audit
a bus station. I think of the raccoon, my roommates clapping,
brandishing. Sidewalks slip into shaded neighborhoods.
Industrial blocks cleave west; saplings bush at car level, block
the eye. Speed limits: 35mph, 45mph. People rattle shopping
carts full of redeemable cans to the bottle drop. No sidewalk,
no landscape buffer. Not a single street-tree to shade the
pavement. Christine texts me a video of a red fox playing in
a vacant parking lot. Hope twinges in her belly. I tick boxes

on a clipboard. 45mph, 50. Across from the bus station, I duck into a rock shop and pay $5 for a fragment of lab-made bismuth. The shop-keep saw somebody struck by a car just last week, a cyclist pulling a full cart. Cans rolled helter-skelter and the rider ran off, *must've had bigger problems*, the rock-seller says. The EAR-ONS cinched ligatures so tight that hands blackened, numbed. Raccoons thrive on proximity with the human habitat. Years back—after I repeated that I wasn't ready—I laid still to wait for a philosopher to finish. The EAR-ONS forced wives to bind their husbands, then re-tied them himself. I guzzle stories; my heart stays raw. The hurt rubs even where I've singed it, methodical, listened again and again for a bone-splinter until I stop flinching. Crunched cans. A man in a red truck plucks the glass from our trash cans twice weekly. The rock-seller installed a fence to stop the cart-pushers from walking across his parking lot. Outside of the rock shop, a wheel jams and cans tumble into the street. Someone screams *Fuck*. That night, I make a map of the bus station and then vape with my future husband in a pioneer cemetery. Christine wants her foot tattooed to resemble a paw. A philosopher's work aims to integrate man with nature. *Isn't this natural*, a philosopher whispered. Christine texts that she saw the mangled corpse of a red fox in the gutter, run over. By then, I had stopped wanting flesh. Sprawl and jut; spruce and swale; second house from the corner, single-story, sliding glass. These skeletons are so old we don't feel disrespectful getting stoned. Shoelace ligatures; fox neck bent all the way back. By then, I want flesh so bad my bones howl. When I get home, the garbage has been collected—bottles and cans picked from the recycling, the chicken's broken body on its

passage to a land-
fill. We will eat her last egg
without knowing it.

WHO CARES ABOUT CONSENT

The world is a dangerous place. Pluckable love
thrums petaled in infinitely tender chests,
taunting predators! Taunted, predators venture
their plenitudes to get some—kingdoms
for mere peaks!—all these sleepless knights
over mere squeezes!—but if her heart's not barbed,
her teeth not sharpened, how's a flesh-starved
architect to avoid erecting his land of plenty
against such a fertile soft? But what's lost
is lost—straw bombardiers pop and scatter
sawdust through the clear air. Silt laced valleys
basically *beg* for settlement; and the river scum
wants and will want forever for an honest sieve,
for cheeks in which to slosh, a throat
in which to gargle. Meanwhile, men astonish
at how wet I get, when it has nothing
to do with them. Watch! my moist weeping,
the geologic seep of me from headwaters
through the plentiful nectar-dripping mythos
of candid romance. Myths of candor—of love
snatched and snatchable—pander
to the masculine impulse to rip fistfuls
of dahlias from neighbors' sockets.
Where is the flaw? I wanted what I took.

I looked at what I saw! Ok. Lenticular defects
seed differences in perspective. Let me get you
your flowchart, let me hold your breath. Let me
wretch on the land-owner's natural altar. Let
me attempt to *get it*, this deposition: how power
slithers through love, eroding its inside
curves, piling sediment against its outside
curves, until force is the more recognizable
signifier for love, looming, even, over affection.
Much how gentry settled where wetness left
remnants, where blessing-fed flowers loudly
begged to be cut, and pluckable love thrummed
thunderous, wonderful, unsafe in all
its scope and detail. I'll never understand it.

PROMISE TO RECEDE

A few hours before I ran into my rapist
at Whole Foods, an older teacher suggested
I bathe myself in the blood of Christ
to rid myself of the curse of the nomad. She had lived
through Hurricanes Betsy and Katrina, learned
to stay on high floors in downtown hotels
whenever floods are forecast. I had drifted
for a decade—from brushfires to typhoons
to hurricanes, nowhere felt like home—so when
my colleague asked why I'd shipped my books
cross-country, I told her about the fortune-teller
who said I'd never settle down. That night, after I ran
into my rapist at Whole Foods, I asked my lover if
it was my fault for saying "no." He asked why was I
foisting this on him. At Whole Foods, my pulse
scaled my esophagus and battered
the backs of my teeth. I don't often open
my mouth for fear of thunder, haven't found
a high up refuge, yet, a place where I can loft
my inconvenient, improbable "no" over
the lapping fantasy that I am, above all else,
a receptacle for sex. That weekend, it stormed.
I stood in the shower while time grated forward
and soap slid off my body and into pipes,

and when I finished and looked out the window,
a foot of water stood in the yard. Wrapped in my towel
I hovered on the front porch, where my roommate smoked
cigarettes and watched the flood inch up our cars,
tip garbage cans, lift oil from asphalt
and ferry the newly potted pomegranate tree
into the street. The storm stalled,
the sick water wouldn't promise
to recede, but I didn't think of the strong women
who lifted their children onto rooftops
or spent wet days dehydrated—I only thought of myself,
ducked behind the kale chips, clawing at
the license to my body. I didn't think of the blood of Christ,
only of my own nomad heart, pumping mud. Nowhere
will be home as long as my body is not mine. I thought
of the desire that surges uninvited
into my every crevice, and wanted nothing
but to lay down under the floodwaters.

DESCRIPTIONS OF HUMAN WOMEN

I.

Breathless—*this is how it ends
for you*—the whisper network
crept, crept

roars today, the *"whores"* swabbed:
their bodies caught you

II.

I admit it—my nipples
are never not
present. No matter

how clothed   how bone tired   how dehydrated
how incapable   of smiling   how tied up

I'm not crying
                 how wired my   politeness into   my body
                     thoughts   my rage   a crime scene
you're crying
                 how violently   dramatic how   slapstick
                 riddled with holes   how holy holy   how often
                                                        I told you
                                              what happened
it's obvious, I've got them
somewhere under clothes.

I promise, I'm less
my body than
the noise I make with it—

III.

Eventually, creations totter off
beyond their authors—they caught him,
Michelle, god bless

the redolent planes, the haystack,
the unmarred flank, the baby
grown and holding her own

body as if
it belongs to her.

IV.

The rape-kit backlog clots. The body
is a crime scene, stripped and swabbed.
Trauma on cotton, the stalked night,
the knocked over table, the mattress
made a hell of, Pollock, blood,
the body become a crime
scene, the body,
her body, her,
my body,
me.

V.

For your amusement—
the fluid Muse—

the blue-sky truth
tooth cracked

and clattering, featherless flap
our falls to earth

where we're nicer to you
in your imagination

where to us you fap
and we're rapturous, glad,
so glad to be touched

like we're flammable,
time-stamped twenty-one,
wonder dilated

violently desirous, wild
for you, for you only

VI.

Pubic hair. Fluids. Chewed nails. Blue eyes.
Ribald. Fine hair. Quiet, lively, chime laugh.
Haven't you? I have. Mild clapper. Pussy
flaps. Trap door—can you believe it?—
the white male feminist says she slammed
it. Treasure chest. Rectum. God bless
the threaded needle, dangling above
the haystack. *The scent pool*. The clues,
the ruses, the truth, at last, the truth.

CONTEXT

Mom dipped her finger in the pool then lifted it, a half-drowned bee crawling up and down her hand, which she rotated, slow, steady, to keep the bee right-side-up while it buzzed and shook water off its wings, unfurled its curlicue tongue, and dragged its tiny bee hands down the length of that tongue again and again, scraping chlorine. Legs dangled, California sun freckled against our shoulders, I saw her as I would see her again and again: the bravest person in the world, loving something misunderstood and making herself vulnerable to its sting. She'd only been stung once but had a scar on her forehead from a dog bite. I crawled out of the womb a month early; I've only grown more distant since. In the summer of 2016, I camped with friends in Grand Isle, Louisiana. Having misunderstood the campground website, we brought Christine's dog. To sneak past campground staff, we wrapped him in a blanket and crept through standing water at the back of the campsites, disturbing a mosquito breeding ground. My legs fuzzed with young mosquitos. My legs constellated with itch. Hyperbole and sensitivity to insect bites—both, inherited. On the eve of my wedding, dad laughed that mom cut back to just one or two cigarettes per day while pregnant with me. Decisions ripple through a scourge, a hive. Before Trump's inauguration, the babes came to our duplex to make yonic protest posters and guzzle boxed wine. The next morning, hungover, we listened to the moans of our neighbor's home birth through the too-thin partition wall. *The baby's first cry*, Ann gasped. Mom's hands have long, brittle nails, but I got my father's stout, strong nailbeds. In her first trimester, she did not know me. Until she tested pregnant, I did not exist. It isn't fair to ask if she was still using, then. On Grand Isle, a storm roiled overnight. My flooded tent wet one side of my body. Six years later, tiny piles of silt still fall from the flaps. A mentor once described babies as flesh plants. In the interests of group survival, she said, our ancestors would smash or abandon them. When I was four, I got caught sucking the smoldering butt of a cigarette. Until she aborted, my friend said drinking wine felt like pouring bleach on a house plant. My mother did not know me, did not know *of* me. It isn't fair to ask if I exist. Feet swinging in chlorine, our joy surged when bee wings blurred into flight—a triumph over the noxious. And still, I left and kept leaving. On a barrier island in Louisiana, we ate savory vegetables from tinfoil packets. Drunk off boxed wine, we screamed every lyric of *Jagged Little Pill* against the too-thin partition wall of the duplex. After the storm flooded us out, the sun rose behind clouds, and the wet sky quivered metallic, the water frothed yellow. We leveled our gazes across the out-of-control gulf, and with ease

we could imagine
animals thrashing under
the oil-sick water.

TO QUANTIFY EXPOSURE

Zone it all. Prohibit the over-cold, the low-
laying and vulnerable. Buffer each watershed tendril
and buffer your loved ones with great care not to
buffer your love. When thinking of the tundra
rest your mind
        on successively less desperate organisms—
polar bears may only hold your attention
for so many seconds, lest the Arctic's
greening and the musk of unfrozen mud
work its way up your ankles.
Do not think of albedo. Do not think
of life as a succession of leavings. Draw
flow diagrams—land's hazards curve
with the earth's contours, land's hazards
have their own gravities. Prohibit the over-dry,
the eroded coast. Build back from the cliff face
                      and factor beauty
      as a colluder with risk. Do not list your lovers
or wonder pointedly whether they think of you; do not
drink away your fear of dying alone. Do not think
about sunk costs, or how ponderously the man-
made habitat has expanded around you, how
roadsound hums you, now, to sleep.

WHO CARES ABOUT CREDIBILITY

The world is a dangerous place. Glacial lakes
spend millennia venturing, dendritic, across continents.
Through my honest
fugues (how many plods I've
                    forgotten, honestly) along
the plaudit-laden way from social chiasma to home
            and safety,
though on my way I lobbed
my breast at
any marked bench
well-laureled, the dew-grass chewed
                    my bare feet, and then:
each day anew, with the newness
of any well-known man who vanishes, readily,
                        into his reputation. The honest truth is
sediment deposits promise nothing. Perspective wends
between eye and imagination,
decussating left-brain/right-body/vice-versa, love in one's eyes,
limit in another's—   yet, not a single separation,
        yet, attention stays   the sole penetrator,
the only genuine force,   course-maker, imploring
speech, language's reach for   content: honesty,
an event's durable facts—lakes leave   salt trails, fail
to enrich downstream valleys,   their rims, give
        silt. My rapes
            taste like this: tongues

slipped from their bodies, flopping down
dust-clotted streambeds,
budded with unspoken fish,
              lists of names,
      stories thick-veined with remorse, poor
judgment, blood ochre, my ripped up
      body frothed, fluttering
across a vascular continent,
           throbbing in all
              its scope and detail.
I'll never
understand it.

THE REDISTRIBUTION OF SEX

Morning trains
announce themselves

through valleys, dissolve
to mist. Fog-clung

lodgepoles ache at their roots.
Miles under, plates writhe.

My flanks slide over
bones. A series of lines

and planes, blood throb,
thrill. I suspected my body

was a debt to be settled.
Trembling bluffs,

unmanned liquefactions,
        sloshing water

        table: I've breasts.
Trains round hills. Chug,

wail. Vestigial
      impulse to wither,

      to hair-wipe a flesh
God's feet. Plates writhe

miles under. Aesthetic capital
      cramps calves, and land

bucks us all, regardless

CLIMATE ADAPTATION PLANNING

Loud leaves, honorable—
proud and on-schedule
deaths that mock
with their sloppy, down-
drift, loose arcs, and the smug
limbs that scratch after
they're shed, and my used up
cuticles dried, peeled off, while
my life is so stuck
to me

Lone gunman,
bone white, so broken—defrag of
national past-
times: first-person
shoot her, laugh at
any lonesome crazy, list
ten women, which
two have been
hurt by their elided
abusers—I have been
raped by an elided agent,
his academic career,
his gilded friends,

his beautiful daughter,
his beautiful bookshelves,
his beautiful bookshelves
silly with women,
who have been
hurt by elided agents,
case studies

in anger's incubation—
women make incredible victims—
live to be lifted in public
estimation, we brave,
we survivors, we denied
our lived experiences,
given the full heft

of events—*she* was raped—
nameless agents, incubated
anger—she *was*
raped—rage grows
a muzzle, a snub
nose—the lone
gunman's wife was she
white was she mother

was she working—
where did her gaze
fall upon the non-body,
the non-agent, did she
take him with her gaze
when she was laid upon

how the leaves lay down
so the canopy can't
snag raindrops
before they reach
the asphalt, and so
how that asphalt gathers
drops through conduits
and runoff traces lands'
crevices, how runoff
cleaves the land and leaves
its lacerations—it was raining
but who rained, tell me
who rained here

WHO CARES ABOUT CAUSALITY

The world is a dangerous place.
The texture of bread depends on the weather,
and weather depends on the taste of bread.
I have tended my thoughts and still they leech, toxic,
into my body. Property washes onshore
for years after a sea-floor fault slips
and cities inundate. Among the debris, a family
finds a soccer ball and sends it back
across the ocean to its owner. Ecosystems
weave through sunk motorcycles, particulate plastic
finds its way back to us, absorbed
in the flesh of fish. Life buds and drips
off pylons, vines the overpass. City in the forest
is the forest in the city—a whole dock washes
onshore from the ocean's
opposite side. Definitional orbit
of parasite and host. Beloved whom
to who? Wind shoves morning
storms into the mountains—the valley blooms
dew hungry, gulps sun. I decide, again,
to survive myself. Whole disciplines
devote themselves to wonder—thumb pages
by thousands—the world itches
in all its scope and detail.
I'll never understand it.

A BURN A BURN

Winds kick the radius of flame
further. An ember can carry half a mile
or more. A small whir of

a bigger fury settles in some elsewhere
brush, nestles in wetless

leaves and renames them so thoroughly
they transmute into change
agents themselves,

like mediated accusations sprout legs
and sprint into silent houses.

Alarms clang. Small whirs

of fury. Call a burn a burn, a spade
a spade, abuse abuse. My parched

land with its wide stance
and its hands open—my parched land
and its wide maw gushing smoke.

The fire front shoves forward. The fire front
is indifferent to decorum,
shoves into December—

the fire, clueless and brutal, colludes
with wind, melts fur, melts skin,

shoves panicked animals
onto our asphalt, our domestic
quietude hurt, alerted.

SENSE

Overnight, winds shifted. Towns woke with sinuses stung
mesquite. Squeak and pop of a chip bag; char on a cut of meat.
When I am told to make sense, it is, generally, someone else's
sense I'm meant to make. After fifteen years vegetarian,
I accidentally swallowed a mouthful of ground beef in a Taco
Bell burrito. Christine, with eyes like fresh-cut grass, asked
me to imagine the cow. Overcome by animal pain, sometimes
she wants to die, but sometimes she wants to live, to rip it all
apart—the last gasps of all these species overlapped with our
lives. And while cows will chew cud and fill bellies well into
the capitalist anthropocene, Christine carries even the thin-
ning shells of young mollusks in her gaze. Sometimes when
her eyes fall on my human body, I can feel the shudder of
ecosystems—there is nothing to do but undress. Her husband
understands, grants us stolen moments in bar bathrooms,
my bed, even once watching. I fail to imagine life with an
exoskeleton—spilled oils gnawing through a fingernail until
the edible pink meat stings against seawater. Does salt sting
a creature steeped in it? Out west, wildfire smoke seeps into
squirrel fur. Odds are, it's not like I imagine—another's sense,
another sensation. Does the gulf's growing dead zone still
taste like ocean? The first time I pressed my mouth against
her, we soaked through parade crowds at golden hour, the
glint of sun on Endymion brass, sucking pungent edibles,

each other, never quite cumming, and even so, she was a cat-
egorical Venus, pearl-luminous woman in cotton underwear,
rising triumphant from between my clamshell legs; an ocean,
holding whole extinctions in her heart. Once, after I tugged
an errant hair from her nipple, we glued store-bought moss to
cardboard, painted our rage while we drank boxed wine and
screamed Alanis Morissette songs with our girlfriends, gluing
silk leaves, sequins. Our friends expected it by then, how we
hovered in bathrooms like eddies, paused to grind against
each other's hands. They must understand the magnetism
of her laugh, how it sweetens the air of a planet we're com-
plicit in trashing. And then I left her, drove from Louisiana
to Oregon, my orange tabby nosing open his canvas carrier
to flinch at the landscape slipping past. I arrived to western
murk, burning. Animals scampered from charred habitats to
manicured lawns. They must understand the rapture of it—
her gaze, how it blisters with mass extinction and scorched
meat, how it steadies and steadies on me—how simple to give
this imperfect part of the problem,

my human, hungry
body, how simple to give
it to her pleasure.

IRRESISTIBLE

The drake's infamous
corkscrew penis
is flashier than the cloaca
and whether it wets or stretches
to accommodate.

I teach my students English words
for herbs, English words
for their uses.
Once, I stuffed a man's pockets
full of rosemary
and the reek of it shook
me open whenever
he looked at me.

A crowd of strangers gathers
at the estuary's edge
to watch the drake circle
and charge the duck.
Her ducklings scatter
and reassemble
like metal shavings
around a magnet. My lovers' hands
find my throat

because I have asked
them to—my body
a bundle—a needle twanged
into a north, twined
sage that smolders. My students crush

mint into honeyed teas
to settle their stomachs, grind
mint into slabs
of meat. I buy my new lover
tamarind paste. If I steady
my gaze, his lip flinches
and he snarls his head back,
equine, offers his own
neck. Some nights
my brainstem dangles

from his grip. I wipe
the names of herbs
off of the white board,
having gathered
their attributes and uses

into the fist
of a word. Irresistible
to give a name and be taken
by one—have I become
pungent? Once, a man
who shook rosemary
from his pockets became enraged,

He raped my friend.
She wrote letters, poems.
She reported him. She told.
We snatched back at pleasure,
wrapped our legs around
each others' faces, dangled
our legs in the filthy water
of Bayou St. John. She appealed,
litigated, loved fiercely,
and nothing, nothing—
nothing affixed a
consequence to him. Our classmates,

colleagues, mentors refused
to latch the word *rapist*
to him. It's irresistible, isn't it?
To give the benefit

of the doubt? Irresistible to doubt
women. My new lover curls
his knuckles around a cue stick

to shoot pool with the rapist—
balls clack. Who could resist
this evasion of names: *rapist,*
rapist, rapist. Licorice
steam eases the swell
of knuckles, my dumb lover
hinged over green felt,
his grip hinged under my jaw,
as I've asked it—*choke*
me—sudden, his eased joints
boil around my throat
like clouds of licorice steam
seep into arthritic hitches,

deliberate. Gathered,
park-goers watch the duckbill
shoved under brown water
by the drake
that boards her,

and I stare at my lover's
hands—angle of the once-
broken pinky, the swollen
joints, the shallow beds
of bitten nails—hands
I've loved, hands I'd recognize
anywhere, hands I'd know
if I severed them.

WHO CARES ABOUT WELLNESS

The world is a dangerous place.
An errant cell, in time, can fell
even a lumbering soul. The hold of a body
by its constituents—keratin, calcium,
gristle, lips. My love hacks
black phlegm into his palm. A long, healthy life
and everyone dying. And still, blooms
persist. They loudly continue, as limbs drip
headstones. As if we were more than kindling.
As if the rich were pinned in the same glass
encasement, as if. As if our bodies weren't
re-gifted. Our droll shoulders
draped in children's labor—let us slip
into a more comfortable idea:
oblivion, every organ a clitoris,
the void unflinching as it inches
up our thighs. So it has come
to this—lists of edible rhizomes
and the brevity of his eyes, while embalmed
bodies wizen and time writhes in its
scope and detail. I'll never understand it.

SPECIMEN

Given: the crisp earth lurches
from its courage. The prism unhinges
its facets, and each of the laugh's halves
slaps you with its staccato. I am here with you,
Planet. My surfaces, too, are impervious.
Laughs splash against my manufactured façade
and cannot work into the dirt of me. Given:
risk elimination splits land in its own
spots. The State is made of flame
hungry stuff; the State is made of taking;
the State rests in a floodplain where
lovers love nakedly while the world's lungs
fill with smoke and water. I've lost my clothes
and my old protocols. My pores clamor
for your vanishing points, for packaged
lathers that might collapse me back
to babyhood. Have you accepted
our ravishing? This anthropocene is a gas!
I laughed about the last black rhinoceros,
then tattled on my last rapist. What good
is a good name if you do no good with it.
We dammed and extracted you—those lapping
waters, that flammable stuff—you asked
for it! Capitalism is like the bad friend

who says you're lucky to get touched at all
with a mug like that—but Planet, I will love you
better. I have seen your red teeth, your phenotypes
collected in jars. My body, too, could use
a treatment plant, a catalogue. My body, my habitat
withered. Given: a list of risky attributes, concretized,
topples. And a laugh has its facets, it's back
to the wall; its glitz is where manufacture stalls.

POST-MORTEM

When they slice open the beached Sperm whale, they find
64 pounds of trash in its digestive system, which doesn't
seem like much for a thirty-ton animal. I dip straws in my
coffee to preserve the sheen of my teeth. House cats aren't
pack animals, but after following rodents to the fringes of
human settlements, they developed several means to express
their needs to people. The whale was severely underweight
for its species. I am not without needs—fragrant shampoos,
a mechanical hum to muffle the nights' sirens and dawns'
honks of lofted waterfowl. A 2018 study finds microplastic
particles in 93% of the 259 bottles of water tested. Conser-
vative estimates of fragment, fiber, pellet, film, foam. Trash
bags and net segments tangled in the whale's intestines;
"a drum among other things." The dumb beat of my heart, my
car inert and scattered with wrappers. I'd famish without
plastic-wrapped vegetables; landfills grow grandiose on the
sheaths of all I've eaten. A drum, a rupture—straw popped
into a juice carton—the silk-like membrane separating
abdominal wall and organs split by sharp plastics the whale
couldn't pass. Aquafina, Dasani, Evian. After an apocalypse:
clangor, then quiet. Symptoms of which include bloat and
nausea. My courage strains to breach convenience, bagged
fruit rots in my office locker. Less than 0.1% of the whale's
body weight was inhabited by trash. A silk-like membrane

separates the constant hum of human comfort from clamor,
then silence. Symptoms of which include thick urine and
thirst. When my orange tabby scratches certain furniture,
I shoo him outside, where he torments the morning birds.
Plastics could not dislodge—I know of my own synthetic
toxins, compulsive thoughts, small rots baggy-trapped, flags
that wind-snap. Symptoms of which include constipation
and vomiting. I'm not more complex than what I'd sacri-
fice—bagged garbage, casual discards; Sperm whales click
in complex codas, clans have dialects. The internet gives us
the sea's receipts—line-tangled rays approaching divers, tern
bodies rotted around bottle-caps, a seahorse clinging to a
Q-tip, adrift. A 2018 study finds plastic fibers in 94.4% of tap
water samples taken in the United States. The vowel sound of
a cat's *meow* hints at its dispatch: long 'o' for loneliness, short
'e' as a greeting. I consider myself fluid, twisting a cotton bud
in my earhole; adaptable, tearing open packaged nuts with my
teeth; sleeping hot, sleeping cold, Schrödinger's low-hanging
fruit, passing a credit-card's worth of microplastic each week
in my feces. A nuisance species inhales its own atmosphere,
itches. Symptoms of which include tenderness; symptoms of
which include genocide, lands milked dry of plenty. Eventu-
ally,

they'll know we were here
by these bright trails of refuse
refusing to rot.

TOPONYMY OF ENTITLEMENT

*

feather-light, the shed exoskeleton
rests inert, while the spider emerges
to exhilarate against air, its raw
flesh unready to weave or snare, newly
bared legs gathered, twitching
until invigorated, in the video,
the people filming thrill
when the huntsman separates
completely from its discarded armor

*

are you comfortable with me sitting this close
                Uncle's breath moistened my neck
        the room hushed, waiting
like I might say no
might hurt
        his feelings

*

three big windows trimmed with cherry
wood wherein grey light suffuses passerby
until dusk when my own lamplight spills
and—greedy, scared—I draw the curtains

*

frogs eat their shed skins, slip the old surface
down their gullets with gawps, gasps, and
centipedes crawl out of themselves, snakes squirm,
cicadas bulge until they split their own backs
and surge pale, wings unfolding

*

uncle widened the V of his legs until his whole side
touched mine and the memory flared—Grandma
yanking us from the bamboo strand, pre-school me
and he mid-twenties, and she shouting
he knows better, that I don't go
alone with him

*

their remnants are everywhere
and when the sun beams
my own skin
motes and drifts
        particulate

*

you know what they say about a precedent
I shed my body into every set of open palms

washed every crevice, I was
runoff gathering an arroyo's mud

*

and they took it without asking,
the men who belonged me to them—

I like to imagine them inhabiting these shed skins,
monstrous, over-jointed, knocking in the wind
I like to imagine me inhabiting their shed bodies

inflating, taking up
every space they've been

WHO CARES ABOUT CONTINUITY

The world is a dangerous place.
The same guardrails that proclaim
safety can swallow
whole families in an instant. I ripped
up these handfuls of grass for you. Blue mist
between graves surges silver—dawn asserts
its gone moment. Blown dandelions—fragmented
wishes slip into dirt, lurk lemon in testament
to an ending dark. But how far the bloom
resurgence feels amid glitter, gasoline,
sirens winding into lungs, hood crunch,
fumbled spine—who years
later would have laughed against a
who years later would have
traveled alone electric to
who years later would have
danced among, laughed electric to
who years later would have
watched water boil while
time writhed in all its scope and detail.
I'll never understand it.

PROPHYLACTIC ROUTINE

for the love of any such Dolores

Sometimes it helps to fasten shut
the eyes, and imagine

the rush of blood amid
the ears as visible

(a festival of red
rivulets; a millennia of tiny hands

trapped in applause). Allow the soft
cosmos of the body

to lurch toward oblivion.
Under the impenetrable

nectar of observation,
the throb rooted

to eternity loosens.
Amaranth collapses.

A flurry of used tissues
settles over the vents.

Time passes: re-rivet open
lids. Perfume stings

the eyes. After millennia,
you notice your hands.

Perhaps preceding days have been
diminutive, given in reverie

of pearl and umbra,
futile hand wrapped
around your cock.

How simple: peel up
a shudder from scraped knees
hovered

above bobby socks. The sweet wink
of guileless light spilled

from an open window,
a silhouette still

in crescendo. Sometimes it helps
to venerate the ooze

toward inertia, to love
the lapse of days as

if you made it. To overcome
inventions, the hunger
for a flame permanently

aglow. Douse the light.

EXIT INTERVIEW

My heaven is a metric one, like my mother's.
Upon arrival, we pray some angel shows us
spreadsheets—charts and maps, graphs
and infographics. How many naps did I take,
over how many hours? How many hearts
did I break, and how long did it take them—
on average—to recover? My mother wants
a count of steps, the volume of bodily
fluids. She wonders what was her top
speed, her total mileage. Incarnate,
she keeps a tally of every mile she's run
since my birth, a tiny tabulation
in the corner of her calendar's squares.
When she hit ten-thousand, her then-husband
bought her a customized trophy. How many
hours, total, will it take us to heal from his
indiscretion? How many children, total,
did he masturbate to, and how vast a network
of hurt was he a dot on? I wonder about the dye-droplet
of my words into the internet's water—if it bled
into how many stranger's homes. How
many people will read my poems? If I
find kind words and diffuse them far,
will I dampen these knots and help them to loosen?

Did his images of little girls come to him
in .zip files, and from where? How many times
does a map of lost-innocence wrap around
the planet. My mother wonders, if every shed skin cell
from her entire lifetime was pressed into a ball,
would it fit in her bedroom. Would the volume of her
exhalations fill a stadium, a cave? The odds
are far from astronomical that every human breath
contains a molecule that once passed
through Christ's lungs. Centuries out
of my tenure on this planet, I want to watch
a geographic time-lapse of my presence here:
the pinprick of the first improbable
cells meeting, my first cry sending traces
of DNA into a hospital room, my steps dragging
my residue all over the planet until I also
become pervasive, maybe constituent enough
to be a moot point, overall.

RUBBERNECK DIORAMA

Father could only Virgil his girl so far through her madness, having—according to the manners of his time—to leave her at the point at which her fascination with her anatomy began to brighten. Had *daddy* always sounded so? There'd be no appropriate holding her, now, no robe-lounging since she'd found her mouth—every mound so flowered.

He sits in a storage tub and it rains only onto him. On the hillsides, cacti glint. From her window, a daughter watches a doll-baby dragged under a sedan's back bumper, but daddy can't hold her hand. She collects her tears in a dropper and, from a great distance, dots them on the dry concrete. Inscrutable Morse code (she has no soul left to save, there is no holding a grown daughter). Down from her tower, she curls in the center of a cul-de-sac, comma, other girls pool around her. Suburban girls in tank tops talk in off-brand slang about babies' soft skulls. Her father watches from his tub—his own peers huddle around pilsners, comparing fears for their daughters—whose is bigger? How strange now does *daddy* sound?

The whole town cranes its neck to make sense of backed-over babies, nice-assed daughters. Mannequins after all, dressed up potential, the unborn tucked into the town's daughters swap cloven feet for sneakers. The girls' wombs echo with the squeak of rubber soles.

There'll be no appropriate holding them now, emboldened by parents' failures to keep babies safe. To grow is to access a flow state from grieving, to blow each moment like a fuse—not to vanquish mishaps in the name of safety but to settle, copacetic, into well-balanced squares. To fold excess possessions ever smaller and set them inside plastic walls. To control the climate. Fathers can only watch

> while all the best laid
> unplanned pregnancies scatter
> through dust-choked gutters—
>
> while his growing girl
> laughs and brandishes her axe
> wound, screams *come at me*

ACKNOWLEDGEMENTS

I created this chapbook from within a network of dynastic colonial privileges—some earned, many not—and with momentum built upon the white supremacist professional culture that simultaneously infantilizes and empowers people who look and move through society like me.

Thank you to Black Lawrence Press and chapbook editor Lisa Fay Coutley for seeing value in this manuscript, for skilled editorial insight, and diligent work to bring the chapbook into being.

Thank you to my parents who, each in their own way, supported a decade of self-inquiry and risk—without the leeway, patience, and capital they have provided, I do not know if I would have written at all. Thank you to my spouse, Riley Clark-Long, for putting in the hard work of supporting creative labor. Thank you to my friends and community; you make hope and creativity possible, and I love you.

Gratitude to the readers, editors, and staff of the following publications, which have previously published poems included in this project:

Barzakh Magazine – "A Burn a Burn"

Berfrois – "Who Cares About Consent"

The Boiler – "To Quantify Exposure"

DIALOGIST – "Exit Interview"

Heavy Feather Review – "Specimen"

Ghost Proposal – "Rubberneck Diorama"

Lunch – "Prophylactic Routine"

Prism Review – "Promise to Recede" (winner of the 2018 *Prism Review* Poetry Contest)

Rascal Literary Journal – "Post-Mortem"

RHINO Poetry – "Toponymy of Entitlement"

The Rupture – "Who Cares About Causality"

Sundog Lit – "Climate Adaptation Planning"

Sycamore Review – "Irresistible"

NOTES

"Descriptions of Human Women" includes fragments of text from Michelle McNamara's *I'll Be Gone in the Dark*.

"Prophylactic Routine" is in conversation with Vladmir Nobokov's *Lolita*.

JESSICA MOREY-COLLINS is a poet and land use planner. Jessica is the author of the chapbook *We Were More than Kindling* (Black Lawrence Press, 2023). Readers can find Jessica's poems in publications such as *Prairie Schooner*, *Pleiades*, *Cotton Xenomorph*, *Maudlin House*, and *Tinderbox*. Jessica earned an MFA in poetry at the University of New Orleans, and a Master's of Community and Regional Planning from the University of Oregon. Her research and writing focuses on organizational, emotional, and community resilience. Jessica has worked as an urban planner, educator, GIS marketer, curriculum developer, and graduate writing consultant. She is a mental health advocate, trauma survivor, and a straight-passing queer, who spends her spare time doting on her angelic friends, handsome spouse, and ridiculous cats.